Echoes In The Quiet

Kassiopia Chaudhuri

BookLeaf Publishing

India | USA | UK

Dedication

To the silent moments that speak the loudest, and to
those who listen with their hearts.
For Mamma and Babaiya, who taught me the language of
love, my husband Indranil, who is my steady anchor in
the quiet,
and my precious daughter Koena, who fills my world
with echoes of joy. This is for you.

Preface

This book is a collection of moments—small, quiet things that often go unnoticed. A breath of morning air, the pause before a goodbye, the way light shifts through a window.

I have written these short poems to capture what it feels like to be here—to love, to lose, to wonder. These poems are reminders that meaning isn't always loud. Sometimes, it's in the spaces in between.

Thank you for reading.

Acknowledgements

This book exists because of the people who have shaped me, in ways big and small.

To my parents—thank you for teaching me the quiet strength of love.

To my husband, my anchor in life.

To my daughter, who reminds me to see the beauty in everyday moments.

And to my friends, mentors, colleagues who have listened, encouraged, and shared their own stories—your presence has made all the difference.

And to every reader who finds a piece of themselves in these words—thank you.

1. Poem #1

Whispers of the Soul

In the quiet, I find myself.
The mirror shows my face,
but not my whole story.
Every crease, every shadow,
a map of roads I've walked
and choices that still follow me.

I see the child I used to be—
curious, full of dreams,
with a ferocious zeal and energy,
and unafraid of the unknown.

Her voice, soft but steady,
asks if I've held onto her wonder
or let it slip away.
Sometimes I know not...

Her eyes hold no blame,
only a reminder:
to keep searching,
to hold on to the spark,

to simply be...
and perhaps a mention of what I used to be...

In her gaze, past and present meet,
and for a moment,
I feel complete...

2. Poem #2

Harbinger of the Night

Night doesn't announce itself.
It just arrives—
not an ending,
just a change.
The air thickens,
the sky turns quiet,
and the world slows down.

She doesn't speak,
but she knows my fears.
She gathers them up,
softly,
like fallen leaves in a breeze.

There's no harm in her stillness,
just a gentle nudge
to remember:
darkness is part of the rhythm,
not the enemy.

The night waits,
patient and steady,

until I find my peace
and the stars start to breathe again.

3. Poem #3

A Landscape of Longing

The ache in my chest doesn't leave,
growing sharper when you're near.
Your laughter belongs to someone else,
but I can't help wishing
it was mine.

I watch you from a distance,
gathering pieces of your attention—
a glance, a smile,
anything you let slip.
I store them away,
tiny moments that feel like treasures.

This love sits quietly inside me,
like a fragile bloom
in an empty field.
It's beautiful,
but it was never meant to last.

4. Poem #4

The Space Between

There's a place where we meet,
not in this world,
but in the pause of a moment—
a silence that feels bigger than time.

Your presence is like a memory,
soft and familiar,
a song I used to know.

Our love lives in fragments—
the glance that lingers too long,
the touch that burns too brightly.
It isn't meant for here,
but for a place where longing ends.

And yet, I carry you with me,
your name etched into my skin,
your memory alive in my chest.
We're like stars in different skies,
always reaching,
never touching.
Still, we shine.

5. Poem #5

The Synergy of Chaotic Order

Chaos arrives first,
wild and untamed,
tearing through what was steady.
It breaks things apart,
but it also sparks something new.

Order follows,
calm and deliberate,
gathering the pieces.
It finds the pattern,
draws lines where there were none,
turns the noise into something whole.

They work together,
always shifting,
always moving.
Chaos brings energy.
Order brings meaning.

We live in their dance,
trying to find our own rhythm,
even when it feels like stumbling.

6. Poem #6

The Seasons of the Mind

Spring is soft,
ideas blooming quietly,
hope humming in the background,
a promise of what's to come.

Summer bursts in,
bright and endless,
every thought full of life.
The mind stretches wide,
its energy unyielding.

Autumn comes slower,
its light golden,
its air thick with reflection.
Memories fall like leaves,
beautiful and bittersweet.

Winter is still,
its silence heavy,
thoughts frozen beneath the surface.
It's a time for waiting,
for quiet renewal.

Each season leaves its mark,
each one necessary.
Together, they shape
the rhythm of who we are.

7. Poem #7

The Legacy of Dreams

Dreams don't die with the dreamer.
They linger, soft but insistent,
in the spaces we leave behind.

Some are planted,
nurtured with hope.
Others drift on uncertain winds,
yet find fertile ground
in the most unexpected places.

Dreams aren't ours alone.
They grow in those who come after us,
reshaped by new hands.

Even forgotten dreams
leave behind their traces—
a foundation, a spark,
a quiet whisper of what could be.

8. Poem #8

The Weight of Silence

Silence carries weight.
It stretches between us,
not empty,
but full of everything we don't say.

I hear your unspoken words
in the pauses,
in the way you hesitate.

We sit together,
wrapped in this quiet,
each glance a question,
each moment heavy with meaning.

Silence holds us,
both a barrier and a bridge.

9. Poem #9

The Duality of Human Nature

We are a mix of opposites,
light and shadow,
kindness and fear.

We heal with one hand,
hurt with the other.

We reach for the good,
but stumble over the dark.
It's not the light or the shadow
that defines us,
but how we move between them.

We are always becoming,
always learning how to rise
and how to fall.

10. Poem #10

The Echoes of the Past

The past doesn't leave.
It lingers,
not as a shadow,
but as a whisper.

Memories come like waves,
some gentle,
others sharp and unyielding.

We carry them,
not as weights,
but as maps—
guides for where we've been
and where we might go.

Healing doesn't mean forgetting.
It means understanding
And with time,
the echoes grow softer,
blending with who we are now.

11. Poem #11

Fragments of Yesterday

It comes without warning,
a song, a scent,
a memory slipping through.

For a moment,
I'm back there—
a golden place,
soft at the edges,
held together by feeling.

I walk through its halls,
touching laughter,
hearing voices
that no longer call my name.

Nostalgia doesn't hurt.
It holds what was,
offering it gently,
reminding me that it mattered.

When it fades,

it leaves behind warmth—
a soft glow that's always mine.

12. Poem #12

The Contradiction of being Human

We're contradictions,
fragile yet unbreakable.
We hold whole worlds inside us,
but still feel small.

We love fiercely,
but with flaws.
We reach for beauty,
but stumble over fear.

And yet,
there is grace in our messiness,
a strange strength
in how we rise after every fall.

We are not perfect,
but we're learning
to find meaning
in the imperfect.

13. Poem #13

A Kaleidoscope of Wonder

The mind is endless,
a canvas for dreams.
In its corners,
hummingbirds fly through starlight,
rivers hum melodies,
and trees hum quiet songs.

We chase fireflies,
dance with shadows,
and laugh at the moon.

There is magic here,
simple and free,
a world where anything can bloom.

14. Poem #14

The Quiet Threads

It's in a smile shared with a stranger,
a glance that says,
"I see you, and I am here too."

It's in the warmth of a hand held,
steady and certain.
It's in the kind eyes of someone
who listens just to understand.

These small, quiet moments
bind us together,
fragile yet unbreakable.

Even in the noise of the world,
they remind us:
we're never alone.

15. Poem #15

Oranges in Winter

The winter sun sits low,
its light soft and golden.
In my hands,
an orange rests,
its skin rough,
its scent sharp and sweet.

I peel it slowly,
the oil bursting into the cold air,
each slice glistening like sunlight.

The first bite is pure joy—
bright, sharp, sweet...
a reminder that even in winter,
there's warmth.

16. Poem #16

Winter's Embrace

The fire crackles softly,
its warmth wrapping around me.
A book rests in my hands,
its worn pages familiar,
its words both an escape and a return.

The scent of woodsmoke mixes
with chocolate and cinnamon.
Each sip of my drink,
a gentle thaw spreading warmth
through chilled fingers.

Outside, the wind howls,
but here, it's quiet.
Contentment settles like a blanket,
stitched with gratitude,
heavy with peace.

17. Poem #17

Fragments of Joy

The first breath of morning,
cool against your skin,
light slipping through the curtains,
patient, unhurried.

The clink of a spoon in the coffee,
steam rising,
warmth settling in your hands.

A stranger's smile—brief,
but enough.
Rain on a warm pavement,
thunder rolling low,
the earth exhaling.

Pages turning,
words pulling you somewhere
you've never been,
but somehow know.
Footsteps in sync with your thoughts,
steady, alive.

Evening hums,
lights flicker on,
the city exhales.
Small moments,
unnoticed,
but full of quiet joy.

18. Poem #18

Eternal in the Silence

Happenstance of crossed paths...
in the quietitude of time,
where words carried weight
and silences spoke volumes.

Their bond was not sought,
yet it found them—
a spark that ignited a fire
too fierce for the lives they lived.

She saw him, not as the world did,
but as he truly was,
his unspoken fears, his hidden light.

And he saw her,
not as a wife, not as a role,
but as the soulmate she would forever be...
twin flames dancing
Their togetherness... awkward in time...

She cherished the moments,
the stolen glances,

the laughter that felt like a secret gift.
She dreamed of building something timeless,
a bridge between their hearts
that no distance could sever.

But he stood on edge,
reticent, restrained,
a man bound...
by the quiet commitments of time...

Though his heart ached,
he held his longing like a secret,
a truth too fragile to speak aloud.
And she, though she longed to stay,
to fight for the connection
that felt like destiny,
could see the quiet pain in his eyes.

So they moved away,
not in anger, but in sorrow,
two ships veering off course,
the stars... between them
a constant, unreachable reminder.

Her world grew quieter.
The echo of his voice lingered,
a shadow across her days.

She carried him in her heart,
as a wound that would never heal.

Some loves are not meant to be lived,
only felt—
a flame that burns within,
casting its light into the corners of the soul,
a reminder of what could have been,
but never was...

And though they moved apart,
their connection endured,
not in the presence,
but in the spaces left behind—
a love unspoken,
unforgotten in time...

19. Poem #19

The Passing light

Time doesn't shout;
it whispers,
softly slipping moments away.

A child's laughter fades,
seasons fold into one another—
green to gold, gold to grey.

We stand in the middle,
holding the present
like it might slip from our grasp.

And maybe that's the point—
to feel the weight of each moment
before it passes.

20. Poem #20

Threads in the Infinite

Under a sky full of stars,
we stand small,
asking big questions.

Who are we,
tiny sparks in the endless dark?
The universe hums in the silence,
its rhythm pulsing in our hearts.

We are made of its dust,
its light,
its infinite wonder.

Maybe we're not meant to know.
Maybe the magic lies
in simply being here—
finite, but full of the infinite.

21. Poem #21

The Journey within

Who am I,
if not the stories I tell myself?
Each name I've worn,
each mask I've held up
to the world.

There's a shadow of who I was
and a light of who I hope to be.
Both pull at me,
reminding me I'm still unfinished.

Change is slow,
like waves reshaping the shore.
What I am now
will fade into memory,
and what I will be
is waiting ahead.

Maybe who I am
isn't a destination,
but the act of becoming.

www.ingramcontent.com/pod-product-compliance
Lightning Source LLC
La Vergne TN
LVHW010838200726
843508LV00012B/2652